The Baby's Own Aesop

Aesop and Walter Crane

Alpha Editions

This edition published in 2021

ISBN : 9789354545863

Design and Setting By
Alpha Editions
www.alphaedis.com
Email - info@alphaedis.com

As per information held with us this book is in Public Domain.
This book is a reproduction of an important historical work. Alpha Editions uses the best technology to reproduce historical work in the same manner it was first published to preserve its original nature. Any marks or number seen are left intentionally to preserve its true form.

Contents

PREFACE	- 1 -
ÆSOP'S FABLES	- 2 -
THE FOX & THE GRAPES	- 3 -
THE COCK & THE PEARL	- 4 -
THE WOLF AND THE LAMB	- 5 -
THE WIND & THE SUN	- 6 -
KING LOG & KING STORK	- 7 -
THE FRIGHTENED LION	- 8 -
THE MOUSE & THE LION	- 9 -
THE MARRIED MOUSE	- 10 -
HERCULES & THE WAGGONER	- 11 -
THE LAZY HOUSEMAIDS	- 12 -
THE SNAKE & THE FILE	- 13 -
THE FOX & THE CROW	- 14 -
THE DOG IN THE MANGER	- 15 -
THE FROG & THE BULL	- 16 -
THE FOX & THE CRANE	- 17 -
HORSE AND MAN	- 18 -
THE ASS & THE ENEMY	- 19 -

THE FOX & THE MOSQUITOES	- 20 -
THE FOX & THE LION	- 21 -
THE MISER & HIS GOLD	- 22 -
THE GOLDEN EGGS	- 23 -
THE MAN THAT PLEASED NONE	- 24 -
THE OAK & THE REEDS	- 25 -
THE FIR & THE BRAMBLE	- 26 -
THE TREES & THE WOODMAN	- 27 -
THE HART & THE VINE	- 28 -
THE MAN & THE SNAKE	- 29 -
THE FOX & THE MASK	- 30 -
THE ASS IN THE LION'S SKIN	- 31 -
THE LION & THE STATVE	- 32 -
THE BOASTER	- 33 -
THE VAIN JACKDAW	- 34 -
THE PEACOCK'S COMPLAINT	- 35 -
THE TWO JARS	- 36 -
THE TWO CRABS	- 37 -
BROTHER & SISTER	- 38 -
THE FOX WITHOUT A TAIL	- 39 -
THE DOG & THE SHADOW	- 40 -

THE CROW & THE PITCHER	- 41 -
THE EAGLE AND THE CROW	- 42 -
THE BLIND DOE	- 43 -
THE GEESE & THE CRANES	- 44 -
THE TRUMPETER TAKEN PRISONER	- 45 -
HOT AND COLD	- 46 -
NEITHER BEAST NOR BIRD	- 47 -
THE STAG IN THE OX STALL	- 48 -
THE DEER & THE LION	- 49 -
THE LION IN LOVE	- 50 -
THE CAT AND VENUS	- 51 -
MICE IN COUNCIL	- 52 -
THE HEN AND THE FOX	- 53 -
THE CAT AND THE FOX	- 54 -
THE HARE AND THE TORTOISE	- 55 -
THE HARES AND THE FROGS	- 56 -
PORCUPINE, SNAKE, & COMPANY	- 57 -
THE BEAR & THE BEES	- 58 -
THE BUNDLE OF STICKS	- 59 -
THE FARMER'S TREASURE	- 60 -
THE COCK, THE ASS & THE LION	- 61 -

THE ASS AND THE LAP DOG	- 62 -
FORTVNE AND THE BOY	- 63 -
THE UNGRATEFUL WOLF	- 64 -
THE FISHERMAN & THE FISH	- 65 -
THE HERDSMAN'S VOWS	- 66 -
THE HORSE AND THE ASS	- 67 -
THE ASS & THE SICK LION	- 68 -

PREFACE

For this rhymed version of the Fables I have to thank my early friend and master **W.J. LINTON**, who kindly placed the MS. at my disposal. I have added a touch here and there, but the credit of this part of the book still belongs to him.

Walter Crane

ÆSOP'S FABLES

THE FOX & THE GRAPES

This Fox has a longing for grapes,
He jumps, but the bunch still escapes.
So he goes away sour;
And, 'tis said, to this hour
Declares that he's no taste for grapes.

THE GRAPES OF DISAPPOINTMENT ARE ALWAYS SOUR

THE COCK & THE PEARL

A rooster, while scratching for grain,
Found a Pearl. He just paused to explain
That a jewel's no good
To a fowl wanting food,
And then kicked it aside with disdain.

IF HE ASK BREAD WILL YE GIVE HIM A STONE?

THE WOLF AND THE LAMB

A wolf, wanting lamb for his dinner,
Growled out—"Lamb you wronged me, you sinner."
Bleated Lamb—"Nay, not true!"
Answered Wolf—"Then 'twas Ewe—
Ewe or lamb, you will serve for my dinner."

FRAUD AND VIOLENCE HAVE NO SCRUPLES

THE WIND & THE SUN

THE WIND and the Sun had a bet,
The wayfarers' cloak which should get:
Blew the Wind — the cloak clung:
Shone the Sun — the cloak flung
Showed the Sun had the best of it yet.

· TRUE STRENGTH IS NOT BLUSTER ·

THE WIND & THE SUN

The Wind and the Sun had a bet,
The wayfarers' cloak which should get:
Blew the Wind—the cloak clung:
Shone the Sun—the cloak flung
Showed the Sun had the best of it yet.

TRUE STRENGTH IS NOT BLUSTER

KING LOG & KING STORK

The Frogs prayed to Jove for a king:
"Not a log, but a livelier thing."
Jove sent them a Stork,
Who did royal work,
For he gobbled them up, did their king.

DON'T HAVE KINGS

THE FRIGHTENED LION

A Bull Frog, according to rule,
Sat a-croak in his usual pool:
And he laughed in his heart
As a Lion did start
In a fright from the brink like a fool.

IMAGINARY FEARS ARE THE WORST

THE MOUSE & THE LION

A POOR thing the Mouse was, and yet,
When the Lion got caught in a net,
All his strength was no use
'Twas the poor little Mouse
Who nibbled him out of the net.

· SMALL · CAUSES · MAY · PRODUCE · GREAT · RESULTS ·

THE MARRIED MOUSE

SO the Mouse had Miss Lion for bride;
Very great was his joy and his pride:
But it chanced that she put
On her husband her foot,
And the weight was too much,
So he died

· ONE · MAY · BE · TOO · AMBITIOUS ·

- 8 -

THE MOUSE & THE LION

A poor thing the Mouse was, and yet,
When the Lion got caught in a net,
All his strength was no use
'Twas the poor little Mouse
Who nibbled him out of the net.

SMALL CAUSES MAY PRODUCE GREAT RESULTS

THE MARRIED MOUSE

So the Mouse had Miss Lion for bride;
Very great was his joy and his pride:
But it chanced that she put
On her husband her foot,
And the weight was too much, so he died.

ONE MAY BE TOO AMBITIOUS

HERCULES & THE WAGGONER

WHEN the God saw the Waggoner kneel,
Crying, "Hercules! Lift me my wheel
From the mud, where 'tis stuck!
He laughed—"No such luck;
Set your shoulder yourself to the wheel."

THE GODS HELP THOSE WHO HELP THEMSELVES

HERCULES & THE WAGGONER

When the God saw the Waggoner kneel,
Crying, "Hercules! Lift me my wheel
From the mud, where 'tis stuck!"
He laughed—"No such luck;
Set your shoulder yourself to the wheel."

THE GODS HELP THOSE WHO HELP THEMSELVES

THE LAZY HOUSEMAIDS

Two Maids killed the Rooster whose warning
Awoke them too soon every morning:
But small were their gains,
For their Mistress took pains
To rouse them herself without warning.

LAZINESS IS ITS OWN PUNISHMENT

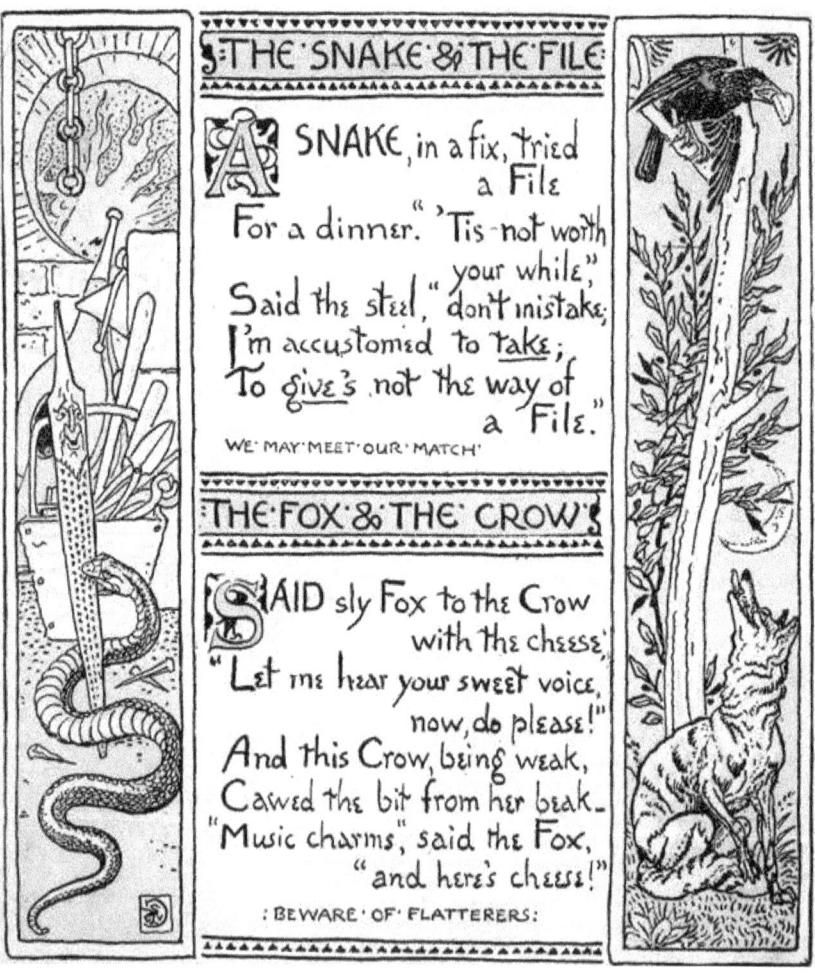

THE SNAKE & THE FILE

A SNAKE, in a fix, tried a File
For a dinner. "'Tis not worth your while,"
Said the steel, "don't mistake;
I'm accustomed to take;
To give's not the way of a File."

WE MAY MEET OUR MATCH

THE FOX & THE CROW

SAID sly Fox to the Crow with the cheese,
"Let me hear your sweet voice, now, do please!"
And this Crow, being weak,
Cawed the bit from her beak_
"Music charms", said the Fox,
"and here's cheese!"

: BEWARE OF FLATTERERS :

THE SNAKE & THE FILE

A Snake, in a fix, tried a File
For a dinner. "'Tis not worth your while,"
Said the steel, "don't mistake;
I'm accustomed to <u>take</u>,
To <u>give's</u> not the way of a File."

WE MAY MEET OUR MATCH

THE FOX & THE CROW

Said sly Fox to the Crow with the cheese,
"Let me hear your sweet voice, now do please!"
And this Crow, being weak,
Cawed the bit from her beak—
"Music charms," said the Fox, "and here's cheese!"

BEWARE OF FLATTERERS

THE DOG IN THE MANGER

A COW sought a mouthful of hay;
But a Dog in the manger there lay,
And he snapped out "how now!"
When, most mildly, the Cow
Adventured a morsel to pray.

· DON'T · BE SELFISH ·

THE FROG & THE BULL

SAID the Frog, quite puffed up to the eyes,
"Was this Bull about me as to size?"
"Rather bigger, frog-brother."
"Puff, puff," said the other,
"A Frog is a Bull if he tries!"

· BRAG IS NOT ALWAYS BELIEF

THE DOG IN THE MANGER

A Cow sought a mouthful of hay;
But a Dog in the manger there lay,
And he snapped out "how now?"
When most mildly, the Cow
Adventured a morsel to pray.

DON'T BE SELFISH

THE FROG & THE BULL

Said the Frog, quite puffed up to the eyes,
"Was this Bull about me as to size?"
"Rather bigger, frog-brother."
"Puff, puff," said the other,
"A Frog is a Bull if he tries!"

BRAG IS NOT ALWAYS BELIEF

THE FOX & THE CRANE

You have heard how Sir Fox treated Crane: With soup in a plate. When again They dined, a long bottle Just suited Crane's throttle; And Sir Fox licked the outside in vain.

·THERE·ARE·GAMES·THAT·TWO·CAN PLAY·AT·

THE FOX & THE CRANE

You have heard how Sir Fox treated Crane:
With soup in a plate. When again
They dined, a long bottle
Just suited Crane's throttle;
And Sir Fox licked the outside in vain.

THERE ARE GAMES THAT TWO CAN PLAY AT

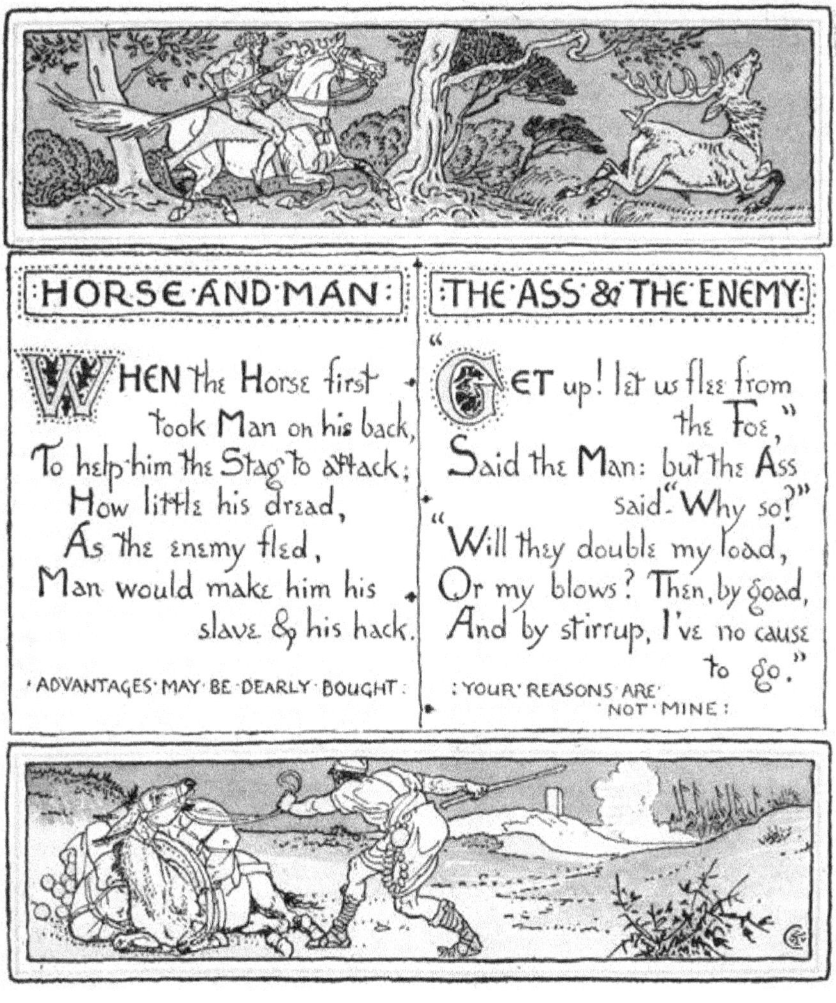

HORSE AND MAN

WHEN the Horse first
took Man on his back,
To help him the Stag to attack;
How little his dread,
As the enemy fled,
Man would make him his
slave & his hack.

: ADVANTAGES· MAY· BE· DEARLY· BOUGHT :

THE ASS & THE ENEMY

"GET up! let us flee from
the Foe,"
Said the Man: but the Ass
said "Why so?"
"Will they double my load,
Or my blows? Then, by goad,
And by stirrup, I've no cause
to go."

: YOUR· REASONS· ARE·
NOT· MINE :

HORSE AND MAN

When the Horse first took Man on his back,
To help him the Stag to attack;
How little his dread,
As the enemy fled,
Man would make him his slave & his hack.

ADVANTAGES MAY BE DEARLY BOUGHT

THE ASS & THE ENEMY

"Get up! let us flee from the Foe,"
Said the Man: but the Ass said, "Why so?"
"Will they double my load,
Or my blows? Then, by goad,
And by stirrup, I've no cause to go."

YOUR REASONS ARE NOT MINE

THE FOX & THE MOSQUITOES

Being plagued with Mosquitoes one day,
Said old Fox, "pray don't send them away,
For a hungrier swarm
Would work me more harm;
I had rather the full ones should stay."

THERE WERE POLITICIANS IN ÆSOP'S TIME

THE FOX & THE LION

The first time the Fox had a sight
Of the Lion, he 'most died of fright;
When he next met his eye,
Fox felt just a bit shy;
But the next—quite at ease, & polite.

FAMILIARITY DESTROYS FEAR

THE MISER & HIS GOLD

HE buried his Gold in a hole.
One saw, and the treasure
he stole.
Said another, "What matter?
Don't raise such a clatter,
You can still go & sit by
the hole."

USE ALONE GIVES VALUE

THE GOLDEN EGGS

A GOLDEN egg, one every day,
That simpleton's Goose used to lay;
So he killed the poor thing,
Swifter fortune to bring,
And dined off his fortune
that day.

GREED OVEREACHES ITSELF

THE MISER & HIS GOLD

He buried his Gold in a hole.
One saw, and the treasure he stole.
Said another, "What matter?
Don't raise such a clatter,
You can still go & sit by the hole."

USE ALONE GIVES VALUE

THE GOLDEN EGGS

A golden Egg, one every day,
That simpleton's Goose used to lay;
So he killed the poor thing,
Swifter fortune to bring,
And dined off his fortune that day.

GREED OVEREACHES ITSELF

THE MAN THAT PLEASED NONE

THROUGH the town
this good Man & his Son
Strove to ride as to please every one:
Self, Son, or both tried,
Then the Ass had a ride;
While the world, at their efforts, poked fun.

YOU CANNOT HOPE TO PLEASE ALL ·· DON'T TRY

THE MAN THAT PLEASED NONE

Through the town this good Man & his Son
Strove to ride as to please everyone:
Self, Son, or both tried,
Then the Ass had a ride;
While the world, at their efforts, poked fun.

YOU CANNOT HOPE TO PLEASE ALL—DON'T TRY

THE OAK & THE REEDS

Giant Oak, in his strength & his scorn
Of the winds, by the roots was uptorn:
But slim Reeds at his side,
The fierce gale did outride,
Since, by bending the burden was borne.

BEND, NOT BREAK

THE FIR & THE BRAMBLE

The Fir-tree looked down on the Bramble.
"Poor thing, only able to scramble
About on the ground."
Just then an axe' sound
Made the Fir wish himself but a Bramble.

PRIDE OF PLACE HAS ITS DISADVANTAGES

THE TREES & THE WOODMAN

The Trees ask of Man what he lacks;
"One bit, just to handle my axe?"
All he asks—well and good:
But he cuts down the wood,
So well does he handle his axe!

"GIVE ME AN INCH & I'LL TAKE AN ELL"

THE HART & THE VINE

A Hart by the hunters pursued,
Safely hid in a Vine, till
he chewed
The sweet tender green,
And, through shaking leaves
seen,
He was slain by his ingratitude.

SPARE YOUR BENEFACTORS

THE HART & THE VINE

A Hart by the hunters pursued,
Safely hid in a Vine, till he chewed
The sweet tender green,
And, through shaking leaves seen,
He was slain by his ingratitude.

SPARE YOUR BENEFACTORS

THE MAN & THE SNAKE

In pity he brought the poor Snake
To be warmed at his fire. A mistake!
For the ungrateful thing
Wife & children would sting.
I have known some as bad as the Snake.

BEWARE HOW YOU ENTERTAIN TRAITORS

THE FOX & THE MASK

A Fox with his foot on a Mask,
Thus took the fair semblance to task;
"You're a real handsome face;
But what part of your case
Are your brains in, good Sir! let me ask?"

MASKS ARE THE FACES OF SHAMS

"THE ASS IN THE LION'S SKIN"

"What pranks I shall play!" thought the Ass,
"In this skin for a Lion to pass;"
But he left one ear out,
And a hiding, no doubt,
"Lion" had – on the skin of an Ass!

· IMPOSTORS ·
GENERALLY · FORGET ·
· SOMETHING ·

THE ASS IN THE LION'S SKIN

"What pranks I shall play!" thought the Ass,
"In this skin for a Lion to pass;"
But he left one ear out,
And a hiding, no doubt,
"Lion" had—on the skin of an Ass!

IMPOSTERS GENERALLY FORGET SOMETHING

THE LION & THE STATVE

On a Statue—king Lion dethroned,
Showing conqueror Man,—Lion frowned.
"If a Lion, you know,
Had been sculptor, he'd show
Lion rampant, and Man on the ground."

THE STORY DEPENDS ON THE TELLER

THE BOASTER

In the house, in the market, the streets,
Everywhere he was boasting his feats;
Till one said, with a sneer,
"Let us see it done here!
What's so oft done with ease, one repeats."

DEEDS NOT WORDS

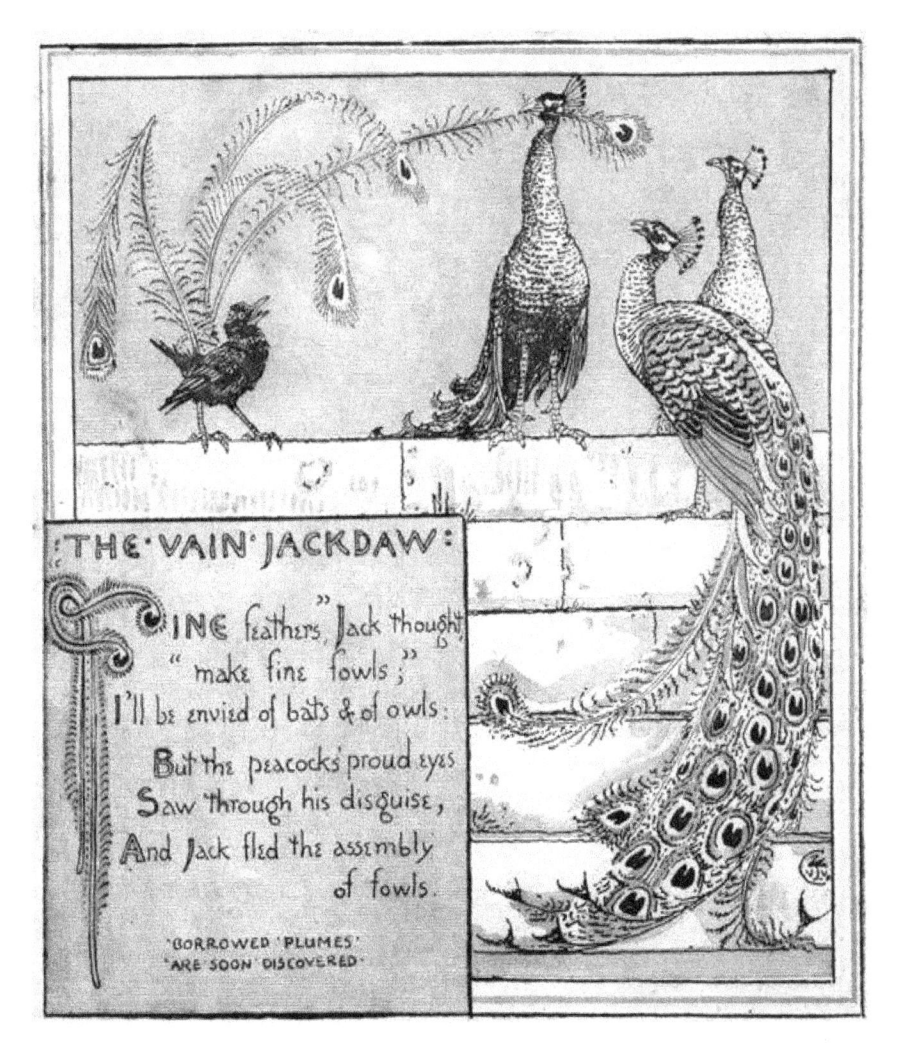

THE VAIN JACKDAW

"Fine feathers," Jack thought
"make fine fowls;"
I'll be envied of bats & of owls.
But the peacock's proud eyes
Saw through his disguise,
And Jack fled the assembly
of fowls.

'BORROWED PLUMES'
ARE SOON DISCOVERED

THE VAIN JACKDAW

"Fine feathers," Jack thought, "make fine fowls;
I'll be envied of bats & of owls:"
But the peacocks' proud eyes
Saw through his disguise,
And Jack fled the assembly of fowls.

BORROWED PLUMES ARE SOON DISCOVERED

"THE PEACOCK'S COMPLAINT"

THE Peacock considered it wrong
That he had not the nightingale's song;
So to Juno he went,
She replied "Be content
With thy having, & hold thy fool's tongue!"

DO NOT QUARREL WITH NATURE

THE PEACOCK'S COMPLAINT

The Peacock considered it wrong
That he had not the nightingale's song;
So to Juno he went,
She replied, "Be content
With thy having, & hold thy fool's tongue!"

DO NOT QUARREL WITH NATURE

"THE TWO JARS"

"Never fear!" said the Brass
to the Clay
Of two jars that the flood
bore away:
"Keep you close to my side!"
But the porcelain replied,
"I'll be smashed if beside you
I stay."

'OUR FRIEND OUR ENEMY'

"THE TWO CRABS"

"So awkward, so shambling
a gait!"
Mrs Crab did her daughter
berate,
Who rejoined, "It is true
I am backward; but you
Needed lessons in walking
quite late."

'LOOK AT HOME'

THE TWO JARS

"Never fear!" said The Brass to the Clay
Of two Jars that the flood bore away:
"Keep you close to my side!"
But the porcelain replied,
"I'll be smashed if beside you I stay."

OUR FRIEND OUR ENEMY

THE TWO CRABS

"So awkward, so shambling a gait!"
Mrs Crab did her daughter berate,
Who rejoined, "It is true
I am backward; but you
Needed lessons in walking quite late."

LOOK AT HOME

BROTHER & SISTER

TWIN children: the Girl, she was plain;
The Brother was handsome & vain;
"Let him brag of his looks,"
Father said; "mind your books!
The best beauty is bred in the brain."

HANDSOME IS AS HANDSOME DOES

BROTHER & SISTER

Twin children: the Girl, she was plain;
The Brother was handsome & vain;
"Let him brag of his looks,"
Father said; "mind your books!
The best beauty is bred in the brain."

HANDSOME IS AS HANDSOME DOES

THE FOX WITHOUT A TAIL

Said Fox, minus tail in a trap,
"My friends! here's a lucky mishap:
Give your tails a short lease!"
— But the foxes weren't geese,
And none followed the fashion of trap.

: YET·SOME·FASHIONS·HAVE·NO BETTER REASON :

THE FOX WITHOUT A TAIL

Said Fox, minus tail in a trap,
"My friends! here's a lucky mishap:
Give your tails a short lease!"
But the foxes weren't geese,
And none followed the fashion of trap.

YET SOME FASHIONS HAVE NO BETTER REASON

The DOG & the Shadow

IS image the Dog did not know,
Or his bone's, in the pond's painted show:
"T'other dog," so he thought,
"Has got more than he ought;"
So he snapped, & his dinner saw go!

GREED IS SOMETIMES CAUGHT BY ITS OWN BAIT

THE DOG & THE SHADOW

His image the Dog did not know,
Or his bone's, in the pond's painted show:
"T'other dog," so he thought
"Has got more than he ought,"
So he snapped, & his dinner saw go!

GREED IS SOMETIMES CAUGHT BY ITS OWN BAIT

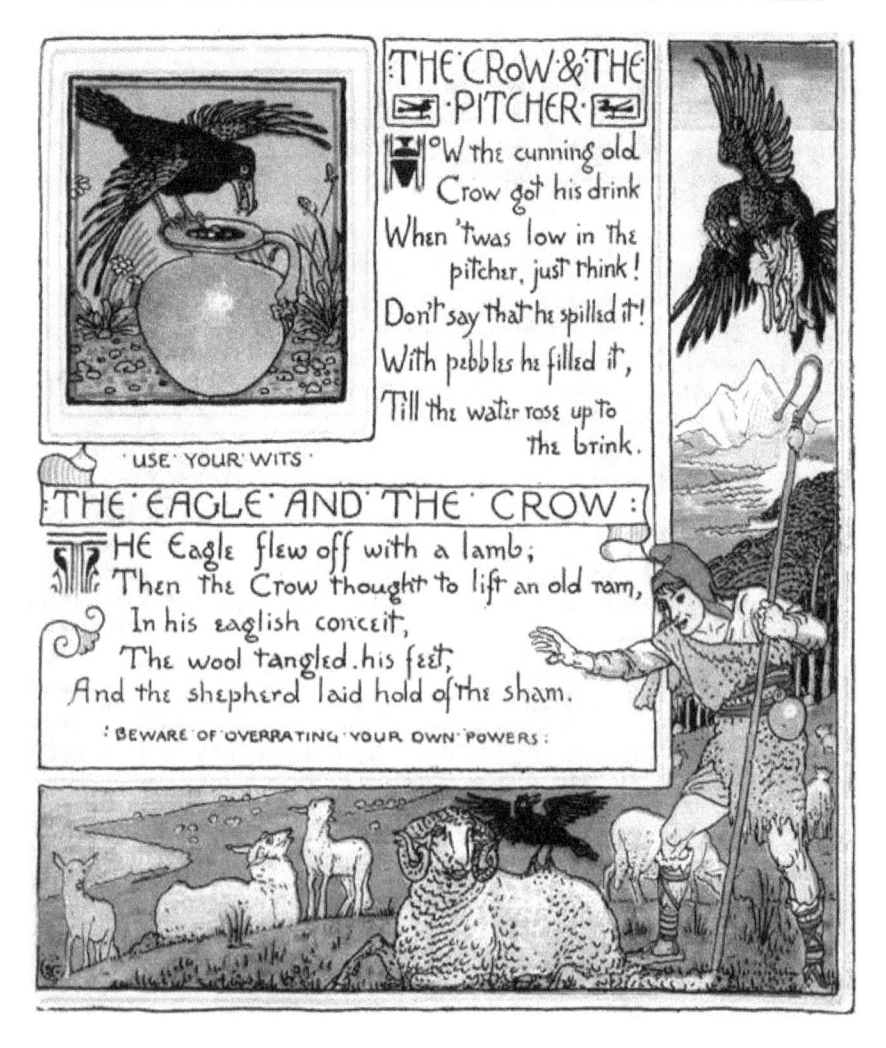

THE CROW & THE PITCHER

How the cunning old Crow got his drink
When 'twas low in the pitcher, just think!
Don't say that he spilled it!
With pebbles he filled it,
Till the water rose up to the brink.

· USE YOUR WITS ·

THE EAGLE AND THE CROW

The Eagle flew off with a lamb;
Then the Crow thought to lift an old ram,
In his eaglish conceit,
The wool tangled his feet,
And the shepherd laid hold of the sham.

: BEWARE OF OVERRATING YOUR OWN POWERS :

THE CROW & THE PITCHER

How the cunning old Crow got his drink
When 'twas low in the pitcher, just think!
Don't say that he spilled it!
With pebbles he filled it,
Till the water rose up to the brink.

USE YOUR WITS

THE EAGLE AND THE CROW

The Eagle flew off with a lamb;
Then the Crow thought to lift an old ram,
In his eaglish conceit,
The wool tangled his feet,
And the shepherd laid hold of the sham.

BEWARE OF OVERRATING YOUR OWN POWERS

THE BLIND DOE

A poor half-blind Doe her one eye
kept shoreward, all danger to spy,
As she fed by the sea,
Poor innocent! she
Was shot from a boat passing by.

WATCH ON ALL SIDES

THE BLIND DOE

A poor half-blind Doe her one eye
Kept shoreward, all danger to spy,
As she fed by the sea,
Poor innocent! she
Was shot from a boat passing by.

WATCH ON ALL SIDES

THE GEESE & THE CRANES

THE Geese joined the Cranes in some wheat;
All was well, till, disturbed at their treat,
Light-winged, the Cranes fled,
But the slow Geese, well fed,
Could n't rise, and were caught in retreat.

BEWARE OF ENTERPRIZES WHERE THE RISKS ARE NOT EQUAL

THE GEESE & THE CRANES

The Geese joined the Cranes in some wheat;
All was well, till, disturbed at their treat,
Light-winged, the Cranes fled,
But the slow Geese, well fed,
Couldn't rise, and were caught in retreat.

BEWARE OF ENTERPRIZES WHERE THE RISKS ARE NOT EQUAL

THE·TRUMPETER·TAKEN·PRISONER

A Trumpeter, prisoner made,
Hoped his life would be spared
He'd no part in the fight, when he said
But they answered him–"Right,
But what of the music you made?"

SONGS MAY SERVE A CAUSE AS WELL AS SWORDS

THE TRUMPETER TAKEN PRISONER

A Trumpeter, prisoner made,
Hoped his life would be spared when he said
He'd no part in the fight,
But they answered him—"Right,
But what of the music you made?"

SONGS MAY SERVE A CAUSE AS WELL AS SWORDS

HOT AND COLD

WHEN to warm his cold fingers man blew,
And again, but to cool the hot stew;
Simple Satyr, unused
To man's ways, felt confused,
When the same mouth blew hot & cold too!

ÆSOP AIMED AT DOUBLE DEALING

HOT AND COLD

When to warm his cold fingers man blew,
And again, but to cool the hot stew;
Simple Satyr, unused
To man's ways, felt confused,
When the same mouth blew hot & cold too!

ÆSOP AIMED AT DOUBLE DEALING

NEITHER BEAST NOR BIRD

A Beast he would be, or a bird,
As might suit, thought the Bat:
but he erred.
When the battle was done,
He found that no one
Would take him for friend at
his word.

BETWEEN TWO STOOLS YOU MAY COME TO THE GROUND

NEITHER BEAST NOR BIRD

A Beast he would be, or a bird,
As might suit, thought the Bat: but he erred.
When the battle was done,
He found that no one
Would take him for friend at his word.

BETWEEN TWO STOOLS YOU MAY COME TO THE GROUND

THE STAG IN THE OX-STALL ❧ THE DEER & THE LION

Safe enough lay the poor hunted Deer
In the ox-stall, with nothing to fear
From the careless-eyed men:
Till the Master came; then
There was no hiding-place for the Deer.

From the hounds the swift Deer sped away,
To his cave, where in past times he lay
Well concealed; unaware
Of a Lion couched there,
For a spring that soon made him his prey.

:AN·EYE·IS·
KEEN·IN·ITS·
·OWN·
·INTEREST·

:FATE·
·CAN·MEET·
AS·WELL·AS·
·FOLLOW·

THE STAG IN THE OX STALL

Safe enough lay the poor hunted Deer
In the ox-stall, with nothing to fear
From the careless-eyed men:
Till the Master came; then
There was no hiding-place for the Deer.

AN EYE IS KEEN IN ITS OWN INTEREST

THE DEER & THE LION

From the hounds the swift Deer sped away,
To his cave, where in past times he lay
Well concealed; unaware
Of a Lion couched there,
For a spring that soon made him his prey.

FATE CAN MEET AS WELL AS FOLLOW

THE LION IN LOVE

Though the Lion in love let them draw
All his teeth, and pare down every claw,
He'd no bride for his pains,
For they beat out his brains
Ere he set on his maiden a paw.

OUR VERY MEANS MAY DEFEAT OUR ENDS

THE LION IN LOVE

Though the Lion in love let them draw
All his teeth, and pare down every claw,
He'd no bride for his pains,
For they beat out his brains
Ere he set on his maiden a paw.

OUR VERY MEANS MAY DEFEAT OUR ENDS

THE CAT AND VENUS

"MIGHT his Cat be a woman", he said:
Venus changed her: the couple were wed:
But a mouse in her sight
Metamorphosed her quite,
And, for bride, a cat found he instead.

: NATURE WILL OUT :

MICE IN COUNCIL

AGAINST Cat sat
a Council of Mice.
Every Mouse came out
prompt with advice;
And a bell on Cat's throat
Would have met a round vote,
Had the bell-hanger not
been so nice.

THE BEST POLICY OFTEN TURNS ON AN IF

THE CAT AND VENUS

"Might his Cat be a woman," he said:
Venus changed her: the couple were wed:
But a mouse in her sight
Metamorphosed her quite,
And for bride, a cat found he instead.

NATURE WILL OUT

MICE IN COUNCIL

Against Cat sat a Council of Mice.
Every Mouse came out prompt with advice;
And a bell on Cat's throat
Would have met a round vote,
Had the bell-hanger not been so nice.

THE BEST POLICY OFTEN TURNS ON AN IF

THE HEN AND THE FOX

THE Hen roosted high on her perch;
Hungry Fox down below, on the search,
Coaxed her hard to descend
She replied, "Most dear friend!
I feel more secure on my perch"

BEWARE OF INTERESTED FRIENDSHIPS

THE CAT AND THE FOX

THE Fox said "I can play, when it fits,
Many wiles that with man make me quits"
"But my trick's up a tree!"
Said the Cat, safe to see
Clever Fox hunted out of his wits.

TRUST TO SKILL RATHER THAN WIT

THE HEN AND THE FOX

The Hen roosted high on her perch;
Hungry Fox down below, on the search,
Coaxed her hard to descend
She replied, "Most dear friend!
I feel more secure on my perch."

BEWARE OF INTERESTED FRIENDSHIPS

THE CAT AND THE FOX

The Fox said "I can play, when it fits,
Many wiles that with man make me quits."
"But my trick's up a tree!"
Said the Cat, safe to see
Clever Fox hunted out of his wits.

TRUST TO SKILL RATHER THAN WIT

THE HARE AND THE TORTOISE

'TWAS a race between Tortoise and Hare,
Puss was sure she'd so much time to spare,
That she lay down to sleep,
And let old Thick-shell creep
To the winning-post first! You may stare.

PERSISTENCE BEATS IMPULSE

THE HARES AND THE FROGS

TIMID Hares, from the trumpeting wind,
Fled as swift as the fear in their mind;
Till in fright from their fear,
From the green sedges near,
Leaping Frogs left their terror behind.

OUR OWN ARE NOT THE ONLY TROUBLES

THE HARE AND THE TORTOISE

'Twas a race between Tortoise and Hare,
Puss was sure she'd so much time to spare,
That she lay down to sleep,
And let old Thick-shell creep
To the winning post first!—You may stare.

PERSISTENCE BEATS IMPULSE

THE HARES AND THE FROGS

Timid Hares, from the trumpeting wind,
Fled as swift as the fear in their mind;
Till in fright from their fear,
From the green sedges near,
Leaping Frogs left their terror behind.

OUR OWN ARE NOT THE ONLY TROUBLES

PORCUPINE, SNAKE, & COMPANY

GOING shares with the Snakes, Porcupine
Said "the best of the bargain is mine."
Nor would he back down,
When the snakes would disown
The agreement his quills made them sign.

HASTY PARTNERSHIPS MAY BE REPENTED OF

THE BEAR & THE BEES

"THEIR honey I'll have when I please;
Who cares for such small things as Bees?"
Said the Bear; but the stings
Of these very small things
Left him not very much at his ease.

THE WEAKEST UNITED MAY BE STRONG TO AVENGE

PORCUPINE, SNAKE, & COMPANY

Going shares with the Snakes, Porcupine
Said—"the best of the bargain is mine:"
Nor would he back down,
When the snake would disown
The agreement his quills made them sign.

HASTY PARTNERSHIPS MAY BE REPENTED OF

THE BEAR & THE BEES

"Their honey I'll have when I please;
Who cares for such small things as Bees?"
Said the Bear; but the stings
Of these very small things
Left him not very much at his ease.

THE WEAKEST UNITED MAY BE STRONG TO AVENGE

THE BUNDLE OF STICKS

To his sons, who fell out, father spake:
"This Bundle of Sticks you can't break;"
Take them singly, with ease,
You may break as you please,
So, dissension your strength will unmake."

STRENGTH IS IN UNITY

THE BUNDLE OF STICKS

To his sons, who fell out, father spake:
"This Bundle of Sticks you can't break;
Take them singly, with ease,
You may break as you please,
So, dissension your strength will unmake."

STRENGTH IS IN UNITY

THE FARMER'S TREASURE

"Dig deeply, my Sons! through this field!
There's a Treasure"—he died: unrevealed
The spot where 'twas laid,
They dug as he bade;
And the Treasure was found in the yield.

PRODUCTIVE LABOUR IS THE ONLY SOURCE OF WEALTH

THE COCK THE ASS & THE LION

THE Ass gave a horrible bray,
Cock crowed; Lion scampered away;
Ass judged he was scared
By the bray, and so dared
To pursue; Lion ate him they say.

DON'T TAKE ALL THE CREDIT TO YOURSELF

THE ASS AND THE LAP DOG

"HOW Master that little Dog pets!"
Thinks the Ass; & with jealousy frets,
So he climbs Master's knees,
Hoping dog-like to please,
And a drubbing is all that he gets.

ASSES MUST NOT EXPECT TO BE FONDLED

THE COCK, THE ASS & THE LION

The Ass gave a horrible bray,
Cock crowed; Lion scampered away;
Ass judged he was scared
By the bray, and so dared
To pursue; Lion ate him they say.

DON'T TAKE ALL THE CREDIT TO YOURSELF

THE ASS AND THE LAP DOG

"How Master that little Dog pets!"
Thinks the Ass; & with jealousy frets,
So he climbs Master's knees,
Hoping dog-like to please,
And a drubbing is all that he gets.

ASSES MUST NOT EXPECT TO BE FONDLED

FORTUNE AND THE BOY

A Boy heedless slept by the well
By Dame Fortune awaked, truth to tell.
Said she, "Hadst been drowned,
I would have surely been found"
This by Fortune, not Folly befel."

FORTUNE IS NOT ANSWERABLE FOR OUR WANT OF FORESIGHT

FORTVNE AND THE BOY

A Boy heedless slept by the well
By Dame Fortune awaked, truth to tell,
Said she, "Hadst been drowned,
'Twould have surely been found
This by Fortune, not Folly befel."

FORTUNE IS NOT ANSWERABLE FOR OUR WANT OF FORESIGHT

THE UNGRATEFUL WOLF:

To the Wolf, from whose throat
      Dr Crane
Drew the bone, his long bill made
                it plain
   He expected his fee:
Snarled Wolf—"Fiddle de dee,
Be thankful your head's out again"

SOME CHARACTERS HAVE NO SENSE OF OBLIGATION

THE FISHERMAN & THE FISH:

Prayed the Fish, as the Fisherman took
Him, a poor little mite, from his hook,
   "Let me go! I'm so small."
      He replied, "Not at all!
You're the biggest, perhaps in the brook."

A LITTLE CERTAINTY IS BETTER THAN A GREAT CHANCE

THE UNGRATEFUL WOLF

To the Wolf, from whose throat Dr Crane
Drew the bone, his long bill made it plain
He expected his fee:
Snarled Wolf—"Fiddle de dee,
Be thankful your head's out again."

SOME CHARACTERS HAVE NO SENSE OF OBLIGATION

THE FISHERMAN & THE FISH

Prayed the Fish, as the Fisherman took
Him, a poor little mite, from his hook,
"Let me go! I'm so small."
He replied, "Not at all!
You're the biggest, perhaps in the brook."

A LITTLE CERTAINTY IS BETTER THAN A GREAT CHANCE

THE HERDSMANS VOWS

A KID vowed to Jove, so might he
Find his herd, & his herd did he see
Soon, of lions the prey:
Then 'twas — "Get me away,
And a goat of the best take for fee."

HOW OFTEN WOULD WE MEND OUR WISHES!

THE HORSE AND THE ASS

OVERLADEN the Ass was. The Horse
Would n't help; but had time for remorse
When the Ass lay dead then;
For he then had to bear
Both the load of the Ass & his corse.

GRUDGE NOT HELP!

THE HERDSMAN'S VOWS

A Kid vowed to Jove, so might he
Find his herd, & his herd did he see
Soon, of lions the prey:
Then 'twas—"Get me away,
And a goat of the best take for fee."

HOW OFTEN WOULD WE MEND OUR WISHES!

THE HORSE AND THE ASS

Overladen the Ass was. The Horse
Wouldn't help; but had time for remorse
When the Ass lay dead there;
For he then had to bear
Both the load of the Ass & his corse.

GRUDGE NOT HELP!

THE ASS & THE SICK LION:

CRAFTY Lion,—perhaps with the gout
Kept his cave; where, to solve any doubt,
Many visitors go:
But the Ass, he said "No!
They go in, but I've seen none come out."

·REASON·FROM·RESULTS·

·THE·END·

THE ASS & THE SICK LION

Crafty Lion,—perhaps with the gout,
Kept his cave; where, to solve any doubt,
Many visitors go:
But the Ass, he said "No!
They go in, but I've seen none come out."

REASON FROM RESULTS

THE END

CPSIA information can be obtained
at www.ICGtesting.com
Printed in the USA
BVHW030058070521
606650BV00005B/760

9 789354 545863